SPACE SCIENCE

GALAXIES

BY BETSY RATHBURN

BELLWETHER MEDIA • MINNEAPOLIS, MN

Are you ready to take it to the extreme? Torque books thrust you into the action-packed world of sports, vehicles, mystery, and adventure. These books may include dirt, smoke, fire, and chilling tales. **WARNING**: read at your own risk.

This edition first published in 2019 by Bellwether Media, Inc.

Library of Congress Cataloging-in-Publication Data

Names: Rathburn, Betsy, author.
Title: Galaxies / by Betsy Rathburn.
Description: Minneapolis, MN : Bellwether Media, Inc., [2019] | Series:
    Torque: Space Science | Audience: Ages 7-12. | Audience: Grades 3 to 7. |
    Includes bibliographical references and index.
Identifiers: LCCN 2018001132 (print) | LCCN 2018007964 (ebook) | ISBN
    9781681036007 (ebook) | ISBN 9781626178595 (hardcover : alk. paper)
Subjects: LCSH: Galaxies–Juvenile literature. | Space sciences–Juvenile
    literature.
Classification: LCC QB857.3 (ebook) | LCC QB857.3 .R38 2019 (print) | DDC
    523.1/12–dc23
LC record available at https://lccn.loc.gov/2018001132

Editor: Rebecca Sabelko   Designer: Andrea Schneider

Printed in the United States of America, North Mankato, MN.

TABLE OF CONTENTS

A STARRY NIGHT

It is a dark summer night. The only light comes from millions of twinkling stars. There are too many to be counted.

A long, white streak stretches across the night. From the horizon, it spans far into the sky. This beautiful streak is part of the Milky Way galaxy!

FUN FACT

ROAD OF MILK

The Milky Way galaxy was named for its white color. Its Latin name means "road of milk!"

WHAT ARE GALAXIES?

From Earth, galaxies look like bright swirls and streaks in the night sky. But they are really huge collections of stars! Some galaxies are home to billions of stars.

Galaxies are found everywhere in the universe. They often exist in clusters that contain thousands of galaxies.

A few galaxies are visible to the naked eye. They stand out in clear, dark skies. Scientists believe there are trillions of galaxies in the observable universe. Many more exist beyond what telescopes can see. The number is too big to be counted!

WHAT ARE GALAXIES MADE OF?

Astronomers believe galaxies formed billions of years ago. The Big Bang left behind a lot of gas and dust. Galaxies formed from these leftover materials.

Over many millions of years, gravity pulled the gas and dust together to form stars. These groups of stars formed galaxies. The Milky Way galaxy has up to 400 billion!

MILKY WAY PROFILE

Size: 588 quintillion miles wide

Number of stars: 100 to 400 billion

Shape: spiral

Name of black hole: Sagittarius A*

Closest neighbors:
- Large and Small Magellanic Clouds, 941 quadrillion miles away
- Andromeda Galaxy, 15 quintillion miles away

Oldest known star: J0815+4729, 13.5 billion years old

Scientists believe each galaxy has a
 at its center. Black holes
are not visible through telescopes. But
their gravity is so strong that scientists
can find them using other tools.

A galaxy's stars travel around its
black hole. It may take millions of years
for a star to make a single orbit.

ILLUSTRATION OF A BLACK HOLE

TYPES OF GALAXIES

All galaxies are made of stars, dust, and gas. But they are not all the same shape. Irregular galaxies are small. They make lots of new stars! Larger galaxies nearby may pull them into strange shapes.

Elliptical galaxies are oval shaped. These galaxies often contain very old stars. They are not as bright as other galaxies.

FUN FACT

ON THE MOVE

Galaxies are always on the move. Some are even moving toward one another! The Milky Way may one day crash into the nearby Andromeda galaxy.

ANDROMEDA GALAXY

A spiral galaxy is shaped like a whirlpool!
It has long arms that swirl out from the galaxy's
center. New stars are found in these arms.
    Each spiral galaxy has a large bulge
near its center. This is where the oldest
stars in the galaxy are found.

TYPES OF GALAXIES

SPIRAL GALAXY

IRREGULAR GALAXY

ELLIPTICAL GALAXY

WHY DO WE STUDY GALAXIES?

Astronomers study galaxies to learn more about the universe. They use instruments like the Hubble Space Telescope to look at faraway galaxies.

They study their sizes, shapes, and ages. They also learn about the materials that make up galaxies. This helps astronomers understand how the universe formed.

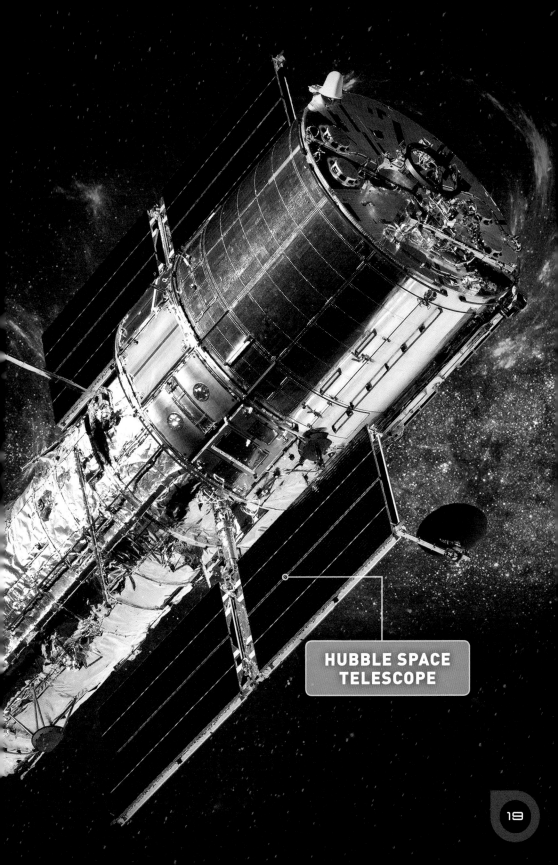

HUBBLE SPACE
TELESCOPE

JAMES WEBB
SPACE TELESCOPE

When it launches, the James Webb
Space Telescope will be the most powerful
telescope ever built. It will help scientists
look further into space than ever before.

The new telescope will find distant galaxies and objects that swirl around them. It may change the way astronomers study the stars!

GLOSSARY

astronomers–people who study space

Big Bang–the explosion that caused the beginning of the universe

black hole–an invisible part of space with very strong gravity

clusters–groups of galaxies

elliptical–oval shaped

gravity–the force that pulls objects toward one another

horizon–the area where Earth seems to meet the sky

observable universe–the part of the universe that astronomers can study with telescopes

orbit–a complete movement around something in a fixed pattern

telescopes–instruments used to view distant objects in outer space

whirlpool–a pool of water that swirls in a circle around a hollow center

TO LEARN MORE

AT THE LIBRARY

Gifford, Clive. *Stars, Galaxies, and the Milky Way*.
New York, N.Y.: Crabtree Publishing Company, 2016.

Hudak, Heather C. *Galaxies*. Minneapolis, Minn.:
Abdo Pub., 2017.

Roland, James. *Black Holes: A Space Discovery Guide*.
Minneapolis, Minn.: Lerner Publications, 2017.

ON THE WEB

Learning more about galaxies
is as easy as 1, 2, 3.

1. Go to www.factsurfer.com

2. Enter "galaxies" into the search box.

3. Click the "Surf" button and you will see a list of
   related web sites.

With factsurfer.com, finding more information is just a
click away.

INDEX